Bb Trumpet/Cornet

Intermediate Level

MASTER SOLOS
by Robert Getchell

Edited by Linda Rutherford

Contents

To access companion recorded performances
and accompaniments online, visit:
www.halleonard.com/mylibrary
Enter Code
2199-8104-5435-9555

ISBN 978-0-7935-9551-8

HAL•LEONARD®

Visit Hal Leonard Online at
www.halleonard.com

Contact us:
Hal Leonard
7777 West Bluemound Road
Milwaukee, WI 53213
Email: info@halleonard.com

In Europe, contact:
Hal Leonard Europe Limited
42 Wigmore Street
Marylebone, London, W1U 2RN
Email: info@halleonardeurope.com

In Australia, contact:
Hal Leonard Australia Pty. Ltd.
4 Lentara Court
Cheltenham, Victoria, 3192 Australia
Email: info@halleonard.com.au

Andantino

musical terms

andantino	in a moderate, easy-flowing tempo
sempre sostenuto	always sustained
espressivo	with expression
poco	a little
a tempo	in tempo, in time, return to the tempo preceding a rit.

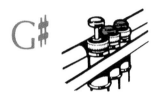

Giuseppe Concone, an Italian pianist and voice teacher, is principally known today for his many vocalises which he composed for his voice students. These are still used by many voice teachers, as well as instrumental teachers, to develop an understanding of the approach to interpretation, tone production, phrasing, and style in the performance of lyrical, melodic pieces.

This "Andantino" has been edited and transcribed for trumpet from one of these vocalises. Although it is extremely simple in its basic melodic and rhythmic structure, it exemplifies the beautiful, rich melodies that were typical of Concone's vocalises and of much of the music of all composers during the Romantic Period (c. 1820-1900).

The very simplicity of this piece makes it, in some ways, more difficult to play than some other solos with more technical demands. The slow tempo and sustained style highlight any defects in the performer's tone quality, breath control, intonation, and phrasing that may frequently be covered up in solos of a faster and more technical nature.

In each solo of this book you will find, in addition to the musical terms indicating the approximate tempo (such as Largo), a more specific metronomic marking, like . . .

M.M. ♩ =60. It may be that, in some of the faster tempos, your finger - or tongue-technique may not yet be developed to a point that permits you to play at the recommended speed, in which case you will have to play at a slightly slower tempo.

This also presents an excellent opportunity for the soloist to employ vibrato which, when used in good taste, adds so much to the beauty of a lyrical piece. Vibrato is the fluctuating or pulsating effect you hear, especially on longer tones. Although the vibrato may be executed in various ways, most trumpet players employ the "hand" or "finger" vibrato, obtained by a very subtle back-and-forth motion of the fingers on the valves. This motion has the effect of alternately increasing and decreasing the mouthpice pressure on the lips (very slightly) and thereby making a slightly higher and lower pitch. Be sure that the fingers do not roll back and forth on the valves, which would have no effect in producing a vibrato. Even on "open" tones, with no valves depressed, the slight friction of one or more fingers just lightly resting on the valve(s) is sufficient to move the instrument back and forth to obtain the desired result. Use the cushiony pad of the finger just underneath the finger nail. Keep the wrist relaxed and think only of the finger-tip moving, rather than the whole hand or arm.

In developing a vibrato, be aware of these three factors:

(1) SPEED OF THE VIBRATO. Set the metronome at 60 and work for a consistent 5 to 6 pulsations per beat.

(2) WIDTH OF THE VIBRATO. The "width" indicates the degree of pitch differentiation above and below the basic pitch. A "too narrow" vibrato will not be heard, while a "too-wide" vibrato is in poor taste and results in intonation problems.

(3) SHAPE OF THE VIBRATO. Work for a smooth wave-like shape (﹏﹏﹏﹏) rather than a jagged saw-tooth shape. (﹏﹏﹏﹏).

The key word is CONSISTENCY — that is, maintaining a steadiness to the speed, the width, and the shape, and keeping them in proper proportion to each other. This is a technique that must be practiced diligently, first on single sustained notes and then gradually incorporated into your melodic playing. Practice sustaining long tones on each note of a scale, literally closing your eyes so your entire concentration is focused on listening to the correct proportion of speed, shape, and width. Do not allow the speed to become slower than five pulsations per second, which would encourage too much "width". Above all, remember that vibrato is meant to enhance and beautify your tone, not to obstruct it.

PREPARATION 1

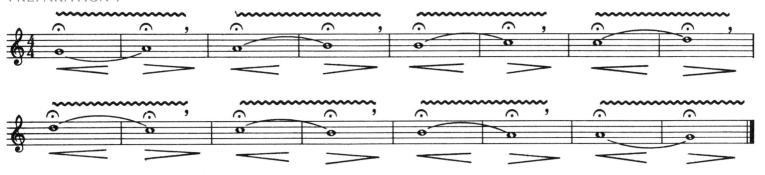

Measures 1-12   The accompanist begins the solo with a four-measure introduction. This should be played in a smooth, sustained style. The slurs in the first four measures indicate this legato style. In measure 4 the accompanist has a "ritard". Measure 5 should be played at the speed which preceded the "ritard". The phrase "sempre sostenuto" (always sustained) in measure 5, indicates that the entire solo is to be played in the same broad, connected style.

The soloist should generally play in four-measure phrases. There are possible exceptions to this, as indicated by the breath mark in parentheses (𝄒). One of these exceptions is the two-measure phrase in measures 9 and 10. In this case, take a breath after measure 10 only if necessary. Remember, when taking a breath between phrases, the note preceding the breath is the one which must be slightly shortened to allow time for the breath. However, try to play this note as broadly as possible so the continuity of the phrase will not be interrupted.

The top space open "E" on a trumpet is, acoustically, a slightly flat note and the first line "E" is an acoustically sharp note. You will be playing many "E's" in this solo because "E" is the dominant or fifth note of the "A" major scale and is an important note. Although the top space "E" can be fingered 1-2, it is recommended that you play it "open", but "lip it up" slightly.

For the first line "E", which is slightly sharp, you will need to lower the pitch slightly either by using the trigger on the first-valve tuning slide or by lipping it down. On all valve brass instruments (including cornets and trumpets), the valve combination 1-3 is very sharp and the valve combination 1-2-3 is extremely sharp. Notes played with these valve combinations are difficult to lip down to pitch without distorting the tone quality. If you have a tuning ring on the third-valve tuning slide, be sure you use it (except in the very fast passages) on any notes employing either of these two valve combinations. The tuning slide should be so free that it literally drops out of the horn if your finger is not in the ring. If this slide is sluggish or "frozen" in the horn, have your instrument repairman buff it down so it will work freely with the slightest flick of your finger. You must use your ear to determine how far the slide needs to be extended to bring the note down to the proper pitch. If you should not have a third-valve tuning ring on your instrument, do the best you can to lip the note down to pitch. Practice the following exercise in the key of A major. Listen carefully to the pitch of the notes, especially the two "E's".

PREPARATION 2

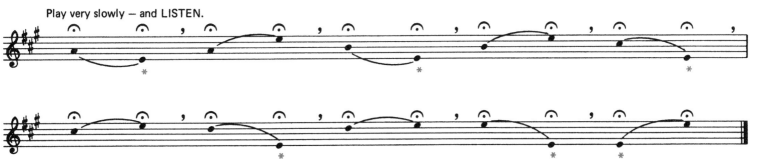

*In the above exercise, if you are using the first-valve trigger, be sure to use it only on the 1st line "E" and not on any other notes employing the first valve.

Be careful in measure 11 that the "G#" is not forced. As in any upper register note, it will be necessary to support the tone with a greater intensity of air — that is, a greater "push" from the abdominal area. Increased air pressure, rather than increased mouthpiece pressure, will insure a free, responsive tone.

Measures 13-28   Again, take a breath in measure 14 only if necessary. Notice the "tenuto" marks in measures 16, 18, and 21. These indicate a very soft, legato tongue, just enough to "dent" the air stream but not actually stop it. A slight "flick" of the tongue on the "shoulder" or projection of the gum just above the upper teeth is all that that is needed for the desired effect. It may help to think

of using a syllable beginning with "D" such as DAH, DUH, or DOO.

Be sure to play the eighth note in measure 20 for its full value before taking a breath.

In measure 25 you have an eighth note triplet which divides a quarter note into three equal parts. $\quad \flat = \sqcap^3$ Practice the following exercise which uses eighth note triplets.

PREPARATION 3

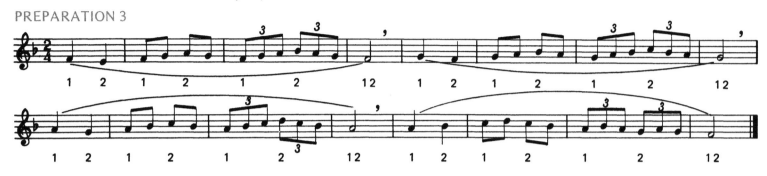

Measures 28-45   The accompanist takes over the melodic line in measure 28. Be sure to bring out the melody in the right hand while the eighth note arpeggiated figures in the left hand act as an accompaniment. In measures 35, 36 and 37, the soloist has a dotted quarter note combined with two sixteenths. This is a rhythm you have already learned with the eighth note divided into

two equal parts. Do not rush these sixteenth notes.

In measures 39, 42, and 43 the dotted eighth and sixteenth rhythmic figure is used. The dotted eighth is equal to three tied sixteenth notes. The following illustrations show you the dotted quarter and two sixteenths rhythm and the dotted eighth and sixteenth rhythm.

ILLUSTRATION 1

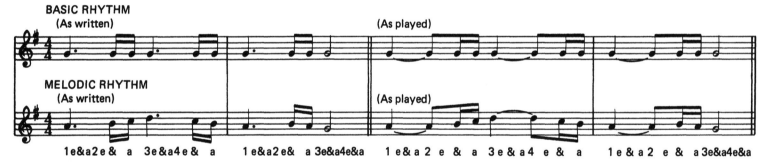

ILLUSTRATION 2

Practice the following exercise to become familiar with both dotted note rhythms and eighth note triplets.

PREPARATION 4

Andantino

Giuseppe Concone
(1810-1861)

Menuet and Ballo

musical terms

andante   **in a moderately slow tempo**
diminuendo (dim.)   **gradually softer**

James Hook, an English organist, composed over 2,000 songs, cantatas, and "catches" (also known as "rounds") during the Classical period of music history (1750-1820). The melodies of this period were less florid and simpler than the melodies of the previous period. Likewise, the harmonies below the melodies were less complex.

The menuet (also minuet) began as an early dance form, is always in triple meter (such as 3/4 or 3/8) and is usually performed at a moderate tempo. It frequently appears as one of the movements in many suites and symphonies dating as far back as the Baroque period (1600-1750).

The accompanist should notice that, as in so many other of the solos in this series, the upper staff changes periodically, back and forth, between the treble and bass clefs. Although this movement presents no technical challenges to the soloist, it does require very careful attention to such important elements of performance as tone quality, control of the tone, an even vibrato, intonation, and proper articulation. These facets of your performance are more "out in the open" in slower tempos than in faster tempos.

In addition to using a very soft-quality legato articulation on those notes which are to be tongued, be especially aware of the intonation on the many low "D's" and "C♯'s" in this movement. Remember to use the tuning slide to help adjust for any notes using the 1-3 or 1-2-3 valve combination. Listen carefully to determine how far the slide needs to be extended to achieve the correct pitch. If you do not have a third-valve tuning ring on your instrument, adjust the pitch by "lipping" the note down.

Measures 1-12   The accompanist begins the solo with a four-measure introduction. Listen to this introduction for the style and tempo. Also use this time to prepare for your entrance. The term "a tempo" in measure 5 instructs you to begin your solo at the tempo which preceded the "ritard" in the accompaniment.

In measure 7, each group of two notes is slurred. Exercise care that the second note of each slur is not played too short.

ILLUSTRATION 3

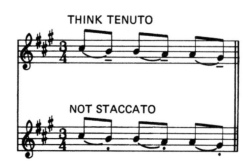

Measures 13-20   This phrase is an "answer" to the melodic idea introduced in measures 5-12. Keep in mind all the elements of good performance as well as the intonation on the low "D's" and "C♯'s". In measure 16, you will notice an "E♯". This is the enharmonic of "F" — that is, it has a different name but sounds the same pitch and is fingered the same (first valve).

In measure 19 there are two small notes before the third beat. These are called double grace or ornamental notes, decorative pitches that in this interpretation are played ahead of the beat. The example below shows how they are written and played.

ILLUSTRATION 4

Ahead of the beat
On the beat

Measures 21-28   Remember to use a soft, legato articulation on any notes that are marked with a "tenuto" mark (—). This phrase has a little more motion because of the smaller note values. Be sure that it does not speed up. In measure 24 there are more double grace notes. Remember that these are played ahead of the beat.

sure to play the slur pattern in measures 31, 33, and 34 as you did before, with the second note of each slur held for its full value. The last note ("A") in measure 32 should be played full value and crescendo smoothly into measure 33, which is the beginning of the final phrase of this movement. Take a full breath in measure 32 in order that you may be able to maintain enough breath to gradually "ritard" and diminuendo to the end of the movement.

Measures 29-36   The original melodic idea returns in measure 29. Notice that the "F♯" becomes "F♯" again. Be

musical terms

allegro	in a fast tempo
senza ritard.	without a ritard
leggiero	lightly and delicately
simile	the same, continue in the same style
molto	much

Daniel Steibelt's name is not too well-known to the musical public today, but during his professional lifetime, he was regarded as highly by his contemporaries as Beethoven. Steibelt enjoyed great prominence as a teacher, a concert pianist, and a composer of many works for keyboard and opera.

Like his contemporary, James Hook, Steibelt's compositions reflect the same delicate, restrained style characteristic of the Classical period. The term "ballo" is an Italian word which implies a light, brisk dance-like piece.

This movement is in 3/8 meter which indicates that there are three beats in each measure and an eighth note receives one beat. Practice the following exercises to become familiar with the different rhythmic patterns used in this movement.

PREPARATION 5

PREPARATION 6

Measures 1-16   The accompanist sets the tempo and the style of this rather playful, light movement. Notice the metronomic marking of ♪=176 which indicates a very fast tempo and therefore should be played lightly and crisply but with much assurance. Soloist, be sure the air is projected into each note so that they are full-bodied and "inflated" with air. There should be a slight distinction between the dynamic level of the first time through the first section and of the repeat, as indicated by the double dynamic markings in measure 9.

One of the most misplayed or misinterpreted articulations by brass players is the "staccato" which is so prominently employed in this movement. Remember that "staccato" means light as well as short, but that the shortness of a staccato varies with (1) the tempo, (2) the respective note value, and (3) the style of the particular piece of music. Brass players too often tend to "punch" the staccato too

heavily with the tongue and/or play it too short with a "pecky" result. This "peckiness" is caused by stopping the note with the tongue too soon, making the note too short, thus the resulting space between notes too long. Be sure to think of one long, sustained, driving column of air, periodically punctuated by the tongue. It is important that, for light staccatos, you use a very short stroke of the tongue, using only the tip and not the entire body of the tongue, which makes for a heavy, clumsy "punchy" sound. This becomes increasingly more important as the speed of the staccato increases — the faster the tonguing, the shorter the stroke of the tongue. Think lightness and delicacy, such as you might expect from a piccolo, flute, or violin playing the same music. Also, think more of the tongue-tip dropping slightly, rather than pulling back, which encourages excess tongue action. Practice the following exercise, first sustaining and projecting a steady stream of air through the instrument; then, while keeping the air stream driving through the horn, suddenly start tonguing into this air stream. Again, while tonguing, always insure that the air stream is moving with the same steadiness and velocity that it was while you were sustaining it. Think the syllable TUH, not TUT while tonguing: TUH-TUH-TUH-TUH — not TUT-TUT-TUT-TUT.

PREPARATION 7

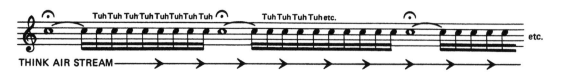

THINK AIR STREAM ⟶   ⟶   ⟶   ⟶   ⟶   ⟶   ⟶   ⟶

Measures 17-24 In measure 17, the dynamic level returns to the "mezzo-forte" (mf) used at the beginning of the first section. Although the staccato marks are not placed under each note, the same light, detached style should continue as indicated by the "simile" in measure 17.

Measures 25-51 In measure 25, the original melodic idea returns. In measure 41 the dotted eighth-sixteenth rhythm should be played lightly, with a very slight shortening of the dotted eighth note (creating a slight space) and a very light articulation on the sixteenth note. Look at the illustration and practice the exercise below to help you in understanding the interpretation of this rhythmic figure.

ILLUSTRATION 5

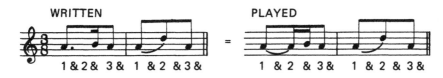

PREPARATION 8

The interpretation of this rhythmic figure is exactly the same when it reoccurs in measure 46.

In measure 51 you will be playing a single grace note. Grace notes are notes which embellish, or decorate, notes on the beat. Thus, the "F#" should be played very lightly and quickly before the "E" which follows it. Practice the following exercise which uses grace notes.

PREPARATION 9

On the beat
Ahead of the beat

Measures 52-64 Beginning with the pick-up note to measure 53, the accompanist answers the four-measure phrase played by the soloist in the preceding four measures. This four-measure phrase should be played with much assurance by the accompanist. The same sequence appears in the following eight measures, where the soloist plays the melody from measures 57 to 60 and the accompanist answers in measures 61 to 64.

Measures 65-82 In measure 65, the original melodic idea introduced by the soloist in measure 9 reoccurs. The fermata (or "hold") in measure 77 should be of short duration with no pause or breath between the fermata and the measure which follows. Notice that measures 81 and 82 are suddenly played much more broadly and with a noticeable "ritard".

Menuet and Ballo

Ballo

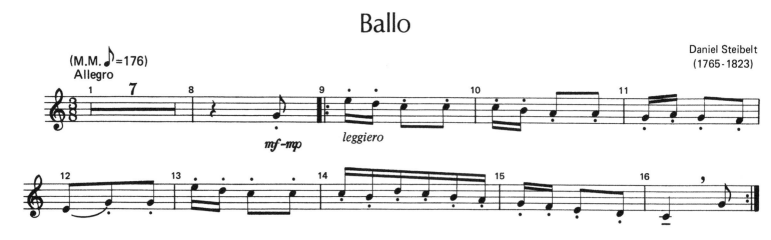

11

Baroque Suite

musical terms

sarabande   **a slow, stately dance in 3/4 meter**
largo   **very slowly**
dolce   **sweetly**

Giuseppe Tartini, a famous Italian violinist and composer, wrote most of his compositions for solo violin or for small string chamber ensembles. This "Sarabande" is taken from one of his many violin sonatas.

The "Sarabande" was a slow, rather dignified dance form associated primarily with the 17th and 18th centuries. This form appeared as the slow movement in suites written for various solo instruments or for small ensembles during this period. In this "Sarabande" you should be especially aware of a clear, singing, free-sounding tone quality.

It is important that any notes which are articulated (tongued) are done so with a very soft-quality attack. As in all performance, the breath must constantly be projected through the instrument in a steady, uninterrupted manner. Especially in the softer passages, the tendency is to let the air "drip" into the instrument which not only makes for a dull, lifeless tone quality, but also encourages the intonation to be flat. Rather, work for a steady, forward movement of the air similar to the constantly moving current in a stream or river.

The following exercise (similar to the opening of the "Sarabande") should be practiced very slowly with a steady air stream.

PREPARATION 10

Be careful that, as the dynamic level increases or decreases, you maintain control of the sound, making sure that it does not become harsh on the one hand, or weak and unsupported on the other.

Always use light mouthpiece pressure. Probably the most common and most dangerous mistake made by brass players — particularly trumpet players — is to rely on excess mouthpiece pressure to insure the response of the upper register. If this becomes a habit and is not corrected early in the player's career, it can spell disaster in the areas of lip endurance and a free, responsive sound in the upper register as the player gradually advances into music which puts more demand on playing in this range. The player must be constantly aware that, as he ascends in range, the center lip muscles (surrounding the lip aperture) gradually increase their "grip" and that the "arm muscles"

do not noticeably increase the mouthpiece pressure on the upper lip. The corners of the mouth should be pulled back and down slightly and remain firm in all registers. "Pressure playing" — that is, using excess mouthpiece pressure — is like putting the upper lip tissue between the jaws of a vise and then tightening the vise. In other words, the tender, sensitive vibrating upper lip tissue is caught between the hard mouthpiece rim on the one side and the hard tooth surface on the other side. As this "vise" gradually tightens (that is, as the mouthpiece pressure increases), this lip tissue becomes so bruised that it cannot vibrate freely and, like any other bruise, requires several days to return to normal. Even the finest professional brass players will use a slight increase in mouthpiece pressure as they ascend into the upper range or as they increase in volume, but the extra amount of pressure is negligible. It is the center lip muscles that actually do the work.

In the following exercise, on the ascending slurs, be aware of the center lip muscles gradually becoming more firm and focusing IN toward the lip aperture, similar to the way the spokes in a wheel all focus toward the hub of the wheel.

Keep the corners of the mouth firm and stationary and do not use any noticeable extra mouthpiece pressure as you ascend to the upper note of the slur. A mirror is an invaluable aid in checking to see that the corners do not stretch outward as you ascend.

PREPARATION 11

Measures 1-8   Because there is no piano introduction to this movement, be sure you have established in your mind, before you start playing, the tempo, the style, and the volume of the opening section. Also, you must have the "feel" of the first note in your lips so that a clean, well-centered sound occurs on the first note. To help indicate the beginning to your accompanist, give a slight downbeat (up-down motion with the bell of your instrument) as a start. The attack for this note should be a "rounded", soft-quality attack. The dynamic level is soft, but your playing should be very free with a well-projected sound. Remember, you are playing to your audience and not to your music stand. Any tongued notes should be very subtly attacked with a little "flick" of the tongue-tip against the "shoulder" above the upper teeth. Remember, the first line "E" is slightly sharp — use your "trigger" or "saddle" on the first-valve tuning slide if you have one — otherwise, lip the note down to pitch. The accompanist should play the quarter note accompaniment very sustained and connected throughout. The crescendo and diminuendo in measures 3 and 4 should be very subtle — just enough for a slight contrast.

Notice the trill in measure 7. A trill is a rapid slurred alternation between two neighboring pitches. In the period in which this solo was written, it was the practice to start the trill on the upper note ("G"). In the following exercises for the trill, strive to maintain an equal response between both notes. Do not allow one pitch to be louder than the other. As the speed increases, be sure that you push the valves all the way down. Also work to keep the notes rhythmically even. Work for a perfect synchronization between the finger movement, the lip movement, and a slight up-and-down motion of the tip of the tongue, similar to trilling when you whistle.

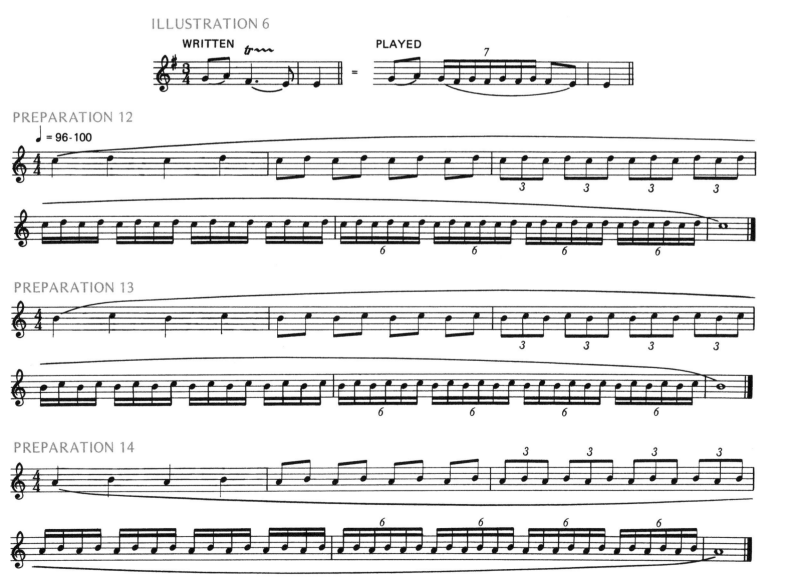

In this exercise ("G" to "A") it is suggested that, as tempo increases, you use 3rd valve on the "A" rather than valves 1—2.

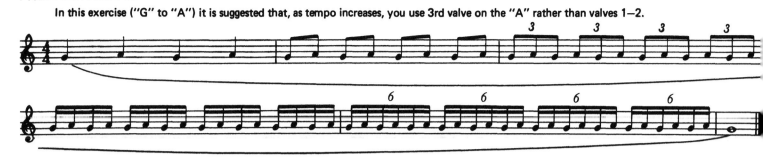

Measures 9-12   In measure 9, do not rush the two sixteenth notes. Without actually dragging them, give them as much value as possible. In measure 12 you'll notice a single grace note before the first beat. Play this grace note very lightly and preparatory to the note which follows it.

Measures 13-16   Be sure that as you ascend in both range and volume to the upper "G" in measure 13, you maintain control of the air stream so that the "G" does not "explode" in a sudden gush of air. Notice the trill in measure 15. This trill is played like the trill in measure 7, starting on the upper note ("B").

ILLUSTRATION 7

Measures 17-20   This four-measure interlude in the accompaniment should be played with much assurance but very warmly. Do not rush the sixteenth notes in measures 17 and 18. The sixteenth "quintuplet" (five-note figure) in measure 19 is an "answer" to the trumpet trill in measure 15. The quintuplet should be played freely and unhurried.

Measures 21-38   The soloist should be especially careful to observe the breath marks as written, using as

little time to breathe as possible to avoid interrupting the flow of the melody. Again, in measure 23 use just enough crescendo and diminuendo to furnish a slight contrast or inflection to the dynamic level. The trill in measure 37 should be executed in the same manner as the trill in measure 15 with the exception that, due to the "ritard", it should gradually broaden out as you approach the fermata in measure 38. Start this trill on the upper note ("G").

musical terms

allegretto grazioso	**at a "moving" tempo and very gracefully and delicately**
poco ritard.	**a little slower**
circa (ca.)	**approximately**

Giovanni Buononcini, the most famous of a family of noted Italian musicians in the 17th and 18th centuries, wrote his first composition when he was only six years old. Although an accomplished cellist, he was best known for his many operatic compositions.

your accompanist begin together. The style and the tempo are in complete contrast to the "Sarabande" movement. In this movement, not only is the tempo quite fast, but the style is very light, delicate, and playful as indicated by the stylistic terms "grazioso" and "leggiero".

Measures 1-8   As in the first movement, there is no piano introduction to set the style and the tempo of this "Rondeau", so take time to "sing" the first few measures to yourself before starting. After you have the tempo set in your mind, give a downbeat to help you and

The articulation mark, shown above or below the quarter notes in measures 1 and 2 (-), indicates a slightly broader staccato than the staccato mark accompanying the eighth notes. However, there should still be a slight space between these quarter notes. Remember to keep the air stream moving with the same steadiness and velocity that it would be if you were sustaining a tone. Think of "lifting" these notes with the breath and separating them with a very light stroke of the tongue. Practice making the distinction between these two articulations in the following exercise.

PREPARATION 16

In measure 3, note the (—) marking above the note "E". This indicates a "tenuto" or full-value interpretation to this note, as contrasted to the bouncy staccatos preceding it. There should be a pronounced crescendo starting at measure 5 and continuing into measure 8. In measure 7 the trill again should start on the upper note ("D"). This is a slightly more difficult trill on the trumpet due to the fact that it "crosses

over" the harmonic series. This trill should end on the third beat of the measure and, unlike the trill in the "Sarabande" movement, should be played as rapidly as possible throughout its duration. If you have difficulty executing a clean trill at this tempo, you may want to use the second figure shown below.

ILLUSTRATION 8

Measures 9-16   Note the softer dynamic marking (mp) in measure 9 (including the "p" for the accompanist). Make a slight distinction in this section, similar to an "echo" of what you just played in the first eight measures. In measure 9, the term "simile" indicates a continuation of the style of articulations employed in the first eight measures. Double grace notes occur before the third beat of measure 15. Remember when these appear here and later, they should be played lightly and preparatory to the beat.

Measures 17-32   Here the dynamic level returns to that used at the beginning, but you should still continue the light, bouncy style of articulation. The "poco ritard" in measure 31 is started by the soloist and continued by the accompanist through measure 32. There should just be a slight hint of a "ritard", then return immediately (in measure 33) to the tempo which preceded the "ritard".

Measures 33-44   In measure 33 a slightly softer dynamic level should be used, but maintain the same style — do not let the tone become weak or thin due to a lack of breath projection behind the tone. In measure 44 try to avoid a breath after the note "B" — rather, phrase this note, with the crescendo into measure 45 without any break. By inhaling fully at the end of measure 40, you should be able to maintain the continuity of the phrase until the next breath at measure 48.

Measures 45-60   In measure 45, the original melodic idea introduced at the beginning of the solo reoccurs for the last time. The interpretation of this section will be the same as the one you used in the first sixteen measures. Measures 59 and 60 should gradually broaden out and the final note in measure 60 diminish in volume as the accompanist plays the last three notes in this measure.

Baroque Suite

Sarabande

Giuseppe Tartini
(1692-1770)

Rondeau

Giovanni Buononcini
(1670-1755)

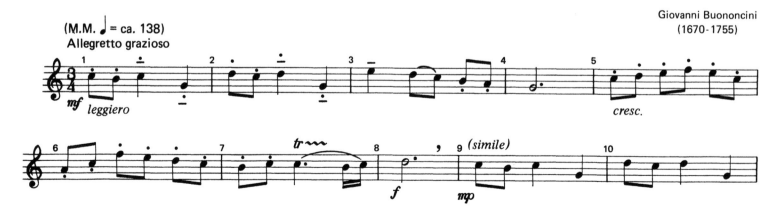

Aria

musical term

a secondary melody played or sung by one instrument or voice which <u>accompanies</u> the principal melody in another instrument or voice

Georg Goltermann, a German by birth, was reared in an entire family of musicians. He learned to play the cello at an early age and, later, toured as a concert cellist. Goltermann was also a composer and a conductor for church and theater musical organizations. Although he is not particularly renowned as a composer, one of his cello concertos is still among the repertoire of many of today's concert cellists. This "Aria" is one of his lesser-known compositions originally written for the cello.

Measures 1-16   The four-measure introduction by the accompanist should be played with much warmth and sensitivity to set the mood for the entrance of the soloist in measure 5. In measure 4, the pianist should gradually diminish the level of volume to that of an accompaniment. As the term "dolce" (measure 5) indicates, the soloist should approach this solo, stylistically, in a very singing, lyrical style. Always strive to phrase this solo in four-measure phrase-groups as indicated by the breath marks. Think of leading constantly from the very first note of each phrase toward the last note of the phrase — in other words, keep the breath projection steady throughout each phrase so there is a continuity. The first note in each phrase is related just as closely to the last note as it is to the second note, in much the same manner that, when speaking a sentence, the thought expressed has a continuity from the first word to the last.

The "Aria" is an excellent example of the music characteristic of the Romantic period (c. 1820-1900). During this period there was a marked departure from the more restrained melodic and harmonic treatment of the music of the earlier Classical period. Musical compositions became more "romantic" and sentimental. The melodies were characterized by much more warmth and emotion, and the harmonies became "lush" and rich through the use of new chords and chord progressions. "Altered" chords (sevenths and ninths) were employed much more freely along with a greater use of chromaticism. This "revolution" in music was also evident in the romantic subjects of the songs and operas composed during this period.

It is extremely important that, from measures 13 through 16, the soloist plays a secondary role and is, in effect, accompanying the pianist who, for these four measures, assumes the role of soloist. The accompanist should noticeably bring out the melody in the right hand while the trumpet player, playing the "obbligato" (or secondary melody), lowers his or her dynamic level to the point that it <u>supports</u>, but does not obscure the principal melody in the piano.

Measures 17-40   In measure 17 the pianist "hands back" the melody to the trumpet soloist. In measure 19, it is extremely important that, because of the slow tempo, the trumpet player utilizes the third-valve tuning ring on the low "C♯". However, it must be moved out very quickly due to the fact that the preceding note ("D♯") is a basically "in tune" note and would be flat if the player were to have the tuning ring out on this note. This requires not only a very free-moving tuning slide, but also perfect coordination between the tuning-ring finger in the left hand and the finger in the right hand executing the valve change. Practice the following exercise to develop this coordination. It is important that:

1. The third-valve tuning slide move so freely that it does not "jar" the instrument when it is pushed out or pulled in.

2. The third-valve tuning slide be extended exactly the right distance to play the "C♯" in tune with the note preceding and following it.

3. The left hand tuning-ring finger and the right hand valve finger are perfectly synchronized in their movement.

PREPARATION 17

(The tuning ring should be extended <u>only</u> on those notes marked with an *.)

PREPARATION 18

In measure 20, be sure to strive for a rich, resonant low "B" by getting the teeth apart, lowering the back of the tongue, and supporting this low note with plenty of air. The melody becomes more dramatic starting at measure 28 where the "forte" dynamic marking should be maintained until the musical tension begins to relax through a gradual "dying away" of both tempo and volume into measure 40. Once again the trumpet soloist assumes a secondary role as the pianist temporarily becomes the soloist.

Measures 40-47   In measure 40, the melody (in the right hand) should be strongly brought out by the accompanist while the right-hand arpeggiated figures are played at a slightly lesser volume.

Measures 48-59   The soloist's entrance in measure 48 should be at a dynamic level that allows for a noticeable crescendo into measure 50 which, along with the ascending melodic line, creates the last dramatic "high point" in the solo. Starting at measure 52, the melody and dynamic level gradually descend into measure 59.

Measures 59-72   This solo comes to a point of rest and could actually end at measure 59. However, the composer has added a short "coda" starting at measure 60 which has the effect of finishing the solo with a little less abruptness. The final note in measure 72 should be extended and brought down to as soft a dynamic level as possible before ending.

Aria

Georg Goltermann
(1824-1898)

MASTER SOLOS
INTERMEDIATE
LEVEL
Edited by Robert Getchell
Performed by Charles Geyer

Trumpet

HAL•LEONARD®

Piano (B♭ Trumpet/Cornet)

Intermediate Level

MASTER SOLOS
by Robert Getchell

Edited by Linda Rutherford

Contents

ISBN 978-0-7935-9551-8

HAL•LEONARD®

Copyright © 1976 by HAL LEONARD LLC
International Copyright Secured   All Rights Reserved

No part of this publication may be reproduced in any form or by
any means without the prior written permission of the Publisher.

Visit Hal Leonard Online at
www.halleonard.com

Contact us:
Hal Leonard
7777 West Bluemound Road
Milwaukee, WI 53213
Email: info@halleonard.com

In Europe, contact:
Hal Leonard Europe Limited
42 Wigmore Street
Marylebone, London, W1U 2RN
Email: info@halleonardeurope.com

In Australia, contact:
Hal Leonard Australia Pty. Ltd.
4 Lentara Court
Cheltenham, Victoria, 3192 Australia
Email: info@halleonard.com.au

Andantino

Giuseppe Concone
(1810-1861)

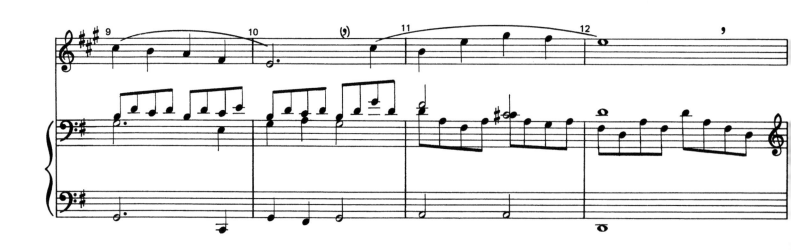

Menuet and Ballo

James Hook
(1746-1827)

8

Ballo

Daniel Steibelt
(1765-1823)

10

Baroque Suite

Sarabande

Giuseppe Tartini
(1692-1770)

Rondeau

Giovanni Buononcini
(1670-1755)

16

Aria

Georg Goltermann
(1824-1895)

Sarabande and Gigue

Jean Rameau
(1683-1764)

Gigue

Johann Pepusch
(1667 - 1752)

Largo and Allegro

Benedetto Marcello
(1686-1739)

29

Allegro

Proclamation, Serenade, and Frolic

Robert Getchell

Serenade

Frolic

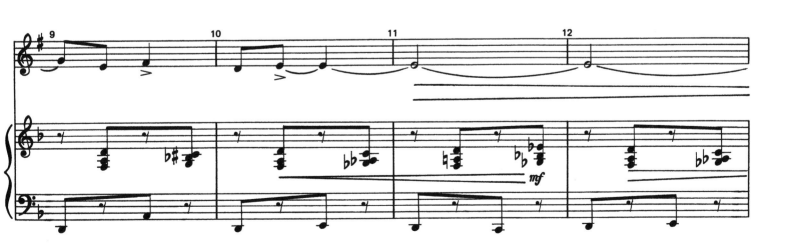

"So Soft the Silver Sound and Clear"

Maurice Monhardt

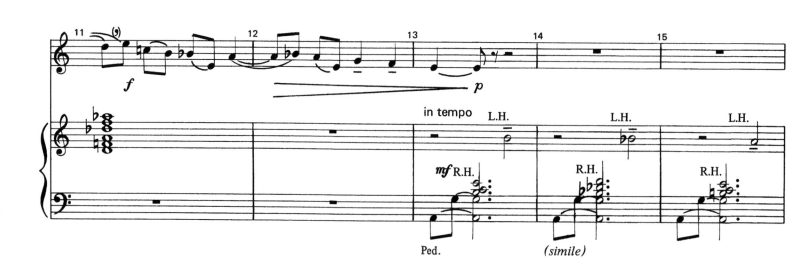

41

43

Sarabande and Gigue

musical term

molto sostenuto   **very sustained and connected**

The "Sarabande" in this solo was composed by Jean Phillippe Rameau, who, like so many of his French musical contemporaries, was a talented organist. With works ranging from ballets to operas, cantatas, and solos for keyboard instruments, he is best remembered for his talents in composition. This "Sarabande" is typical of the slow, rather dignified dance form associated primarily with the 17th and 18th centuries.

Measures 1-4   The accompanist should remember that, in keeping with the style of the Baroque period, the trill in measure 3 should start on the upper of the two notes ("F"). Also the trill should end on beat 3 on the note "E".

The soloist should use a very soft-quality attack on all notes in this movement which are tongued, including those with legato marks (—) such as in measures 5, 9, 13, etc. Concerning the legato style of articulation used in this movement, and in all solos of a slow, lyrical nature, the syllable normally recommended for this articulation

is one which begins with a "D" such as D(AH), D(UH), D(OO), etc. The reason for using the "D" (DAH, DUH, etc.) for legato tonguing is that the tip of the tongue is up on the "shoulder" of the mouth, just above the upper teeth, where it permits a more gentle release of the air stream on attacks. The "AH", "UH", "OO", etc. will be determined by the register in which the music occurs. An upper-register note will call for more "arch" in the back of the tongue, whereas a note in the lower register of the instrument requires that the back of the tongue be un-arched, or low in the mouth, such as "UH" or "AH". In other words, it is not possible to obtain a rich, resonant low-register note, such as low "G" on the trumpet, with the back of the tongue in an arched position.

In the following exercise for legato articulation, picture in your mind Diagram A where the sustained air stream is slightly "dented" but not stopped. Remember to use a syllable that begins with "D" for this style of articulation. Compare Diagram A to Diagram B where the air stream is momentarily interrupted due to the tongue-tip stopping the air stream directly behind the upper teeth. Use a syllable beginning with the letter "T" to obtain this effect.

ILLUSTRATION 9

DIAGRAM A

DIAGRAM B

PREPARATION 19

Measures 5-12 Think in four-measure phrases with an uninterrupted continuity of the melodic line throughout each four-measure phrase. The "Sarabande" provides another excellent opportunity to employ a very subtle vibrato to enhance the beauty of this simple melody. In measure 12, accompanist please note that, after the repeat, the upper (right-hand) staff changes from treble to bass clef.

It was a common practice in music of this period to add some embellishments on the repeat of a section. In the repeat of measures 5-12 slight changes have been made in measures 8 and 12. The rhythm of measure 8 was altered slightly and one note added. The illustration below shows what the soloist played on the cassette.

ILLUSTRATION 10

In measure 12 a double grace note was added.

ILLUSTRATION 11

Measures 13-24 The soloist must be sure to use the third-valve tuning ring on the "C♯" in measure 16. This will necessarily have to be executed smoothly and quickly, as the tuning ring should not be extended on the preceding note, "D♯". Again, a reminder that the tenuto mark (−) under the note "B" in measure 16 is to remind you to not

"cheat" or shorten the note any more than necessary before taking your breath for the following phrase. Notice the trills in measures 19 and 23. Remember to start the trill on the upper note ("G") and to start rather slowly and gradually increase the speed into beat 3 where the trill ends.

musical term

allegro non troppo   **fast, but not too much**

Johann Christopher Pepusch was born in Germany, but, when still a young man, established residence in England where he obtained a Doctor of Music degree from Oxford University. Although he was a church organist, he devoted most of his time to composing liturgical music and operas. Later, as conductor of the orchestra at Drury Lane Theater in London, he composed music for their theatrical productions.

The "Gigue" (or, in English, "Jig") is a lively dance in 6/8 meter and was popular with composers as far back as the sixteenth century. Being in a fast tempo, it is counted with two beats to the measure. Remember you should "feel" the main beats (or tap your foot) on what would be beats 1 and 4 of a slow 6/8 meter.

ILLUSTRATION 12

| Fast | 1 | | | 2 | | | 1 | | 2 | | | 1 | | | 2 | | | 1 | | 2 | | |
| Slow | 1 | 2 | 3 | 4 | 5 | 6 | 1 | 2 3 4 | 5 | 6 | 1 | 2 | 3 | 4 | 5 | 6 | 1 | 2 | 3 | 4 5 6 |

Measures 1-8   The accompanist sets the style and tempo in the eight-measure introduction. All of the eighth notes should be played very lightly and detached with the exception of measure 7 where the notes in the left hand should gradually broaden due to the "ritard".

Measures 9-16   Note the "leggiero" term indicating a light, playful style in both the solo and the accompaniment. The only exceptions would be in measures 9 and 13 in the solo part where the notes should be played broadly and smoothly. In measure 14, an optional breath mark has been placed for the soloist. Breathe here only if necessary.

To correctly interpret the rhythm in measure 15, and in following measures, the player must be sure to slightly shorten the dotted-eighth note, creating a slight space between it and the sixteenth note which follows. Also, the sixteenth note should be played very late in this tempo (much like a grace note). Play this rhythm as if it were written as shown below.

ILLUSTRATION 13

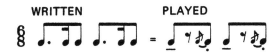

Practice the following exercise which uses this rhythm.

PREPARATION 20

Measures 17-33   In measures 20 to 23, note the octave skips on "E" in the solo part and the answering octave skips on "D" in the left hand of the piano. The pianist should bring out these octaves a little more than the rest of the accompaniment. There should be a very noticeable "ritard" starting at measure 32 (on the repeat) and continuing through the second ending in the piano.

Sarabande and Gigue

Jean Rameau
(1683-1764)

Gigue

Johann Pepusch
(1667-1752)

Largo and Allegro

musical terms

largo   **very slowly and broadly**
doloroso   **sorrowfully, somberly**

Benedetto Marcello was a highly educated Italian whose musical career was temporarily interrupted when his father insisted he pursue the law profession rather than music. He was subsequently appointed to various high government positions, but, upon his father's death, Marcello returned to music where he became a highly respected composer of both vocal and instrumental music. Much of his music is

still performed today, either in its original form or in the form of transcriptions for various solo instruments.

The "Largo" is written in the key of E minor. This means that the song is built around a minor scale. You've already studied major scales and key signatures. Look at the illustration below.

ILLUSTRATION 14

E Major

E Minor

You'll notice that compared to the E major scale, this minor scale has lowered third, sixth, and seventh steps. It is also common for the sharp seventh ("D♯" in this key) to be used in a melody. These changes are the reason a composition in a minor key sounds different than a composition in a major key.

Every attempt should be made to observe the phrasing (breath marks) as written, to avoid any interruption of the melodic line within each phrase. Try to project warmth and mellowness in your tone while retaining beauty and sensitivity in your interpretation. Be sure to use a very subtle vibrato throughout the solo.

Measures 1-12   The term "doloroso" in measure 1 should not mislead the soloist in the stylistic interpretation of this first movement. Even though this term means sorrowfully and somberly and the key is different, this movement should project a sweet, singing lyrical quality in keeping with the beauty of the melody. Remember to give a downbeat to help you and your accompanist begin together.

The 3/2 meter signature may be a new experience for you. Notice that the metronomic marking indicates the half note as the basic unit of counting — think three beats (or half notes) per measure.

ILLUSTRATION 15

As Written: (Measures 1-5)

As Counted:

Even though you should be thinking only three beats (or three basic counts) per measure, you should be subconsciously feeling the "ands" (or second halves) of each beat. For practice reading 3/2 meter, try the following exercise.

PREPARATION 21

Another rhythmic figure that may be new to you is the quarter note triplet which occurs in measures 6, 7, and 9. This rhythm is similar to the eighth note triplet you've already learned except the half note is divided into three equal parts. $\quad$ Practice the following exercise which will help you feel the rhythm of the quarter note triplet as it is used in this movement.

PREPARATION 22

The accompanist should remember that "sempre molto sostenuto" means "always very sustained". The entire accompaniment in this movement should be played in the connected style indicated in measures 1 and 2. Even though the slurs are periodically broken from one group of notes to another, there should be no noticeable break (or space) between these slurred groups, except where there is a breath mark. As an example, the dotted half note "B" in measure 2 should be full-value and lead directly into the quarter note "F" following it. This "F" should be started with a legato attack. The "poco crescendo" starting at measure 6 should be very subtle and just enough of a gradual increase in volume for a slight contrast. Play the quarter note triplets in measures 6 and 7, and following, very "lazily" and unhurried.

Measures 13-22   In measures 17 and 21, remember that the trill should start on the upper note ("G") and, being in a slow tempo, should start and gradually accelerate to the end of the trill on beat 3.

musical terms

scherzando   **lightly, playfully**
subito (sub.)   **suddenly, immediately**

Measures 1-20   The soloist starts this movement, unaccompanied, in a very light, capricious style with a rhythmic and melodic figure which is answered by the accompanist in measure 2. It is therefore important that you mentally sing the first three or four measures to have the tempo, style, and volume well in mind before you start. A feature of this entire movement is the "echo" effect. Sometimes the soloist echoes himself and other times the accompanist furnishes the echo effect. The first such example is in measure 5, where the accompanist echoes the melodic and rhythmic figure just played by the soloist in the preceding measure. Be sure that the dynamic level drops to the point where an echo results, but the "echo" should still be played with lightness and assurance and in the same detached, bouncy style that characterizes the entire movement. In measure 7, and following, the soloist has a series of slurred sixteenth notes which occur periodically throughout the solo. The smoothness and evenness with which these sixteenth notes are executed depends on how accurately the fingers and the lip flexibility are synchronized. The following two exercises are designed to develop a finger fluency in rapid slurred sixteenth note runs. The first example is written in a diatonic (or scale-wise) motion and the second utilizes the skip of the third as is found in the solo.

PREPARATION 23

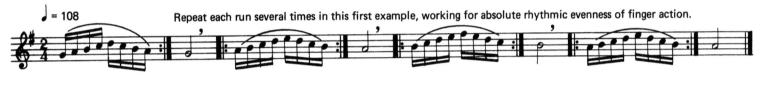

$\quad$ = 108   Repeat each run several times in this first example, working for absolute rhythmic evenness of finger action.

PREPARATION 24

$\quad$ = 108

Measures 21-26   In measure 21, the same rhythmic idea that opened the solo is used again, except that instead of being a descending melodic idea (as in the opening) this one occurs as an ascending melodic figure. Note, in measure 25, the pianist again echoes the trumpet melodic idea of measure 24.

trumpet echo. The soloist must be sure, in these echo sections, not to lose support of the tone nor allow the style of the echo sections to be different than the original statement.

Measures 27-46   From measures 27 through 33, the soloist has a very "busy" section with the sixteenth note runs. Practice these many times, individually, so you can play them with fluency and ease. It is important that, for these sections to "flow" evenly and without hesitation, your lips and fingers literally have these runs "memorized". In measures 35, 40, and 45, the soloist echoes himself, as indicated by the "subito piano" (sub. p). In the first two instances, the accompanist also plays an echo part to the

Measures 47-62   Starting at measure 47, the solo starts to build to a climax by means of a gradual crescendo accompanied by a gradual ascending melodic line. In measure 54, the final echo in the piano appears. There should be no lessening of tempo when approaching the first ending. However, the second time through this repeat section, there should be a very abrupt and pronounced "ritard" starting with the first note in the second ending and continuing to the very end. The trill in the second ending should be lengthened to match the "ritard".

Largo and Allegro

Benedetto Marcello
(1686-1739)

Allegro

Proclamation, Serenade, and Frolic

The titles of each of the three movements of this solo reflect the style or personality of each respective movement and the soloist should endeavor to project this style by the way he interprets the music. As an example, a light frivolous, playful song would usually call for a light, delicate staccato, while a pompous, grand, triumphal song would normally be interpreted by giving more weight to the attacks (known as "breath accents"). A very sweet, singing, lyrical piece would demand a very soft-quality, legato style of articulation. The kind of articulation (or tonguing) which the performer employs determines, more than any one factor, the style or personality of a given piece of music. This is why it is so important that you gradually practice and perfect a wide "repertoire" of articulations and then use the particular style of articulation that associates itself with a given style in a piece of music.

musical terms

bravura	**boldly, aggressively**
rubato	**in a free, flexible interpretation — not to be played in a strict, rhythmic style**
caesura (//)	**a slight delay before the next entrance**

The term "Proclamation", in this setting, implies that the performer is making a very important announcement, delivered with pomp and much assurance, and in a triumphal, authoritative manner. As the opening measure indicates ("bravura"), it should be played very boldly and with much aggressiveness. Think of "ff" (fortissimo) as being not "loud" but very "full". In other words, do not allow the dynamic level of the opening notes to result in a "blatty" quality. The rhythmic figure in the opening measure is one which you may not yet have encountered. Although it does not have to be played in a strict tempo, it is basically interpreted in the manner outlined in the following illustration.

ILLUSTRATION 16

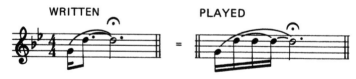

Practice the following exercise which uses the rhythm illustrated above.

PREPARATION 25

In the beginning of the solo the dotted eighth note is tied to a dotted half note. This "D" with a fermata should drive through to the end of the measure with no diminishing volume. The accompanist should note the fermata (hold) over the half rest in measures 1, 2, and 3, which indicates the trumpet's "D" should sustain for some time before the piano entrance on the third beat. The piano entrance in measure 1, as in the case of the solo part, should be very heavy and percussive. Measure 2, in both the solo and the accompaniment, should be an exact duplication of measure 1, with the exception that it should be much softer, as if you were hearing in the distance an echo of measure 1.

In measures 3 and 4, the soloist should play the notes very flexibly, rhythmically speaking, and definitely not in the strict rhythmic manner in which the note values are written. In measure 4, the tenuto (–) marks under the eighth note triplets indicate a broader, full-value interpretation to the notes as you go into the "ritard". The final measure (measure 6) should be played very sweetly and in a "reflective" manner, reminiscent of the very first two notes played at the beginning of the movement.

It is difficult for the brass player to sustain a note softly, such as in measures 2 and 6, for a long period of time and still maintain a stable pitch and tone quality. Be sure that the breath is moving steadily on these soft sustained notes and that the breath does not "drip" into the horn. The following long tone exercise (which should be a part of the "daily diet" in the trumpet player's practice sessions) is very effective in helping to develop a control of tone and intonation at varying degrees of volume. Literally close your eyes and "look" at each note "through your ears" as you crescendo and diminuendo being sure that, as the dynamic level increases, the tone quality does not become loud and raucous and that the pitch does not vary; also that, as the dynamic level decreases, you do not allow the tone quality to become "sickly" and "pinched" from lack of steady projection of air through the instrument. Actually, as the dynamic level approaches the "pp", you should feel an even greater "push" and firmness in the abdominal area to insure that the air stream does, in fact, continue moving at a fast rate of speed, keeping the tone healthy and well-supported by the breath.

PREPARATION 26

(Very long holds. LISTEN as you gradually crescendo and diminuendo that you maintain a consistency in pitch, tone quality, and general control of the tone and breath.)

musical terms

sereno	**in a serene, peaceful style**
meno	**less**

Here, again, the personality of this movement is reflected in the title. A "Serenade" is a sweet, peaceful song somewhat similar to a lullaby and should be played in a very relaxed, placid manner with much emphasis on a clear, pure tone quality. This movement presents another opportunity for the soloist to employ the vibrato.

Measures 1-6   The accompanist, throughout this movement, (with the exception of the last note in measure 10 and the first note in measure 11) uses a very smooth, connected style. The term "simile" in measure 3 indicates a continuation of the same "slurred" style of the first two measures. The soloist will frequently encounter, in this movement, the note low "D". This is another sharp valve combination (1-3) on which the third-valve tuning ring should be extended. Be sure these low "D's" are adjusted down to pitch either with the third-valve tuning ring or by lipping down. The accompanist should note, in measures 5 and 6, and similar places throughout the solo, the crescendo and diminuendo. These occur in those sections where the soloist is sustaining a note and the piano should become more prominent and momentarily assume the solo role.

Measures 7-10   The sixteenth notes in measures 7 and 9 should be played very broadly and unhurriedly, due to the style and tempo of this movement. In measure 9, the (–) indicates a very soft legato articulation.

Measures 11-18   In this section, starting with the heavier and louder pick-up note to measure 11 in the piano, the playing should become more brilliant and excited by means of a slightly higher dynamic level and a slightly higher register. However, continue to employ a very sustained, legato style of articulation where indicated. In measure 14, the "meno" means, in this case, "less motion" or a slight "ritard". The four measures from 15 through 18 are an "answer" to the four-measure phrase which preceded (measures 11-14) and should be interpreted in the same manner.

Measures 19-29   In measure 19, the original melodic idea presented in measure 3 returns again and the interpretation of this section all the way through measure 26 should be identical to the opening section. From measure 27 to the end of the movement, a slight "echo", reminiscent of measures 25 and 26, should be effected by the soloist, with the note "D" gradually dying away into "nothing". Do not diminuendo too softly, too soon — save some for the final measure where the sustained "D" should maintain its "body" as it gradually fades away.

musical terms

cantabile   **in a singing, lyrical style**
giocoso   **jokingly, playfully**

The term "Frolic" is self-explanatory. In other words, "have fun" playing this movement. It should be played in a very light, capricious manner both by the soloist and the accompanist.

Measures 1-22   In the four-measure introduction, the accompanist should play the eighth notes very short and metallic, with a very noticeable crescendo into measure 3 and just as noticeable a diminuendo into measure 5. The soloist should play the eighth notes throughout with a very clean, light staccato articulation.

This may be your first exposure to shifting meters. If so, do not let it frustrate you at first, for with a little practice, you will quickly learn to feel the shifting pulses which are so much a part of the music of modern composers. As is indicated between measures 6 and 7, the eighth note remains the same value as you change from 2/4 meter to 3/8 meter, and this will remain true throughout the solo as the meters change back and forth. Practice the following exercises to accustom yourself to the shifting meters. Be sure the accents are brought out where indicated.

PREPARATION 27

♩ = 132 (♪= ♪) Tap your foot each place an accent occurs.

As written

As played

In measures 10 through 13, the accompanist makes a very noticeable crescendo and diminuendo underneath the sustained trumpet note. Soloist, be sure to observe the accent marks. These are very important in furnishing the rhythmic "drive" which is so essential to this movement. From measures 19 through 22, the accompanist should again make a pronounced crescendo and diminuendo.

Measures 33-46 Here the fast-flowing rhythm and tempo continue but should change, stylistically, to a very liquid, flowing style completely in contrast to the brittle staccato which preceded it. The accompanist should play very smoothly and connected while the soloist changes to a singing, cantabile style.

Measures 23-32 In measures 24 through 28, accompanist notice the accent (∧) markings. This symbol indicates a sharply-accented, very short note. It is important that these be observed to support the accents in the solo part. In measures 29-32, the accompanist again should observe the crescendo and diminuendo.

Measures 46-51 Both the soloist and accompanist should drive from here to the end with a big crescendo, ending in measure 50 with very sharply-accented, tongued notes by the soloist, and very short, percussive chords by the accompanist.

Proclamation, Serenade, and Frolic

Robert Getchell

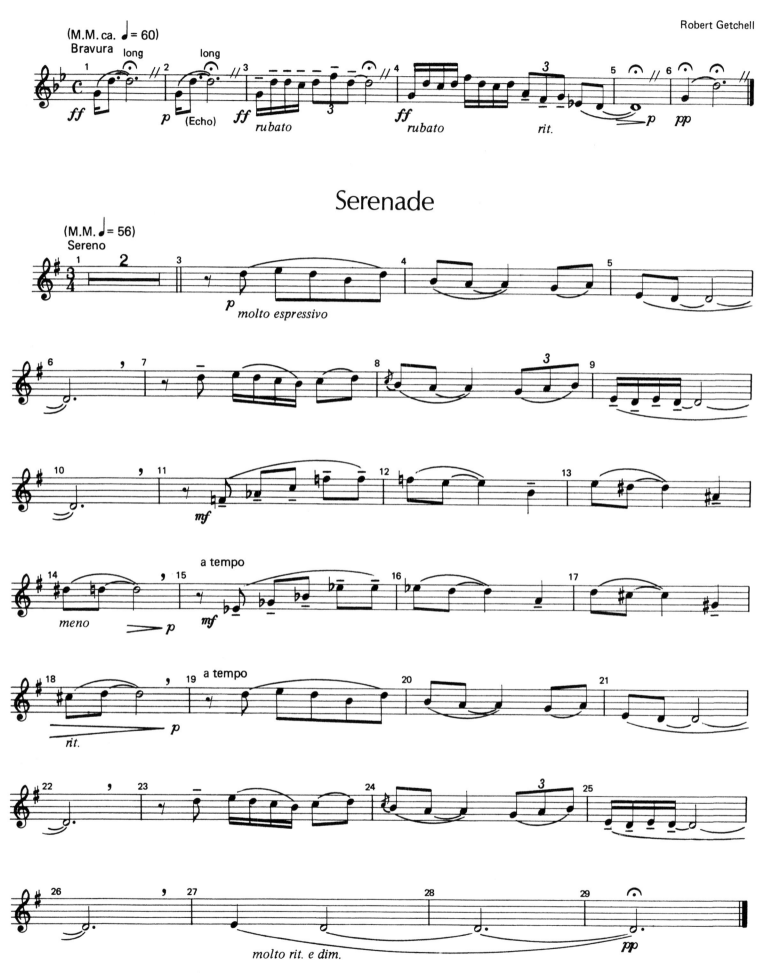

Serenade

Frolic

"So Soft the Silver Sound and Clear"

new note

A

Maurice Monhardt is a contemporary composer and has many published works ranging from symphonies, choral and band compositions to works for chamber ensembles and solo instruments. This solo was written especially for this series.

This solo is an excellent example which incorporates some of the more contemporary styles of composition into a solo that is very playable by the novice soloist and accompanist. The solo does not demand of the player any of the extremes of range and technique but does require a maturity of style, interpretation, and musical sensitivity that is very much within the reach of the young soloist aspiring to perform some of the more-advanced contemporary works available to him.

You will note the absence of any key signatures. This is because it is not written in any given key (or tonality) — rather, it is "atonal", meaning there is no definite "key center" throughout the solo. This, as in so many of the other atonal compositions, will result in many so-called "dissonances" in the piano accompaniment. Lacking a key signature, "accidentals" (sharps and flats) are placed before any notes requiring them.

The entire solo should be performed in a very lyrical, singing style with close attention to the dynamic contrasts which are so extremely important in creating a musically-satisfying performance.

Measures 1-12 Another characteristic of many 20th-century compositions that will be found in this solo is the absence of the lower number in the meter signature. The soloist and accompanist should imagine the number "4" underneath each of the meter numbers $\left(\frac{3}{4}, \frac{2}{4}, \frac{5}{4}, \text{etc.}\right)$.
In other words, the speed of the quarter note remains the same in each meter change.

The accompanist will note that a rhythmic figure characteristic of this solo is the quarter note triplet. In this triplet three quarter notes are divided evenly over the period of two beats (equivalent to a half note). The following illustration will help to clarify the interpretation of this rhythm as it occurs in the pick-up to measure 1 and also in measure 2 of the accompaniment. You will note the second note of the triplet occurs just <u>before</u> beat two, and the third note of the triplet occurs just <u>after</u> beat two. Practice tapping your foot slowly in an even two beats per measure while tapping, with your finger, the three quarter notes evenly divided within these two basic beats in each measure. Because the accompaniment only has the quarter note triplets, cues are shown in the solo part. These will help the soloist enter correctly in measure 4.

ILLUSTRATION 17

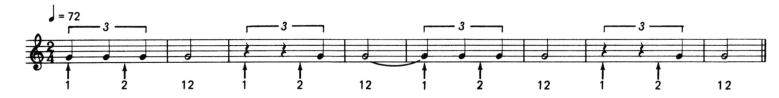

In the four-measure introduction, and throughout the solo, the accompanist should play with a very sustained, connected style.

The term "freely", indicated at the beginning of the solo, means that both the soloist and the accompanist are allowed to take certain minor rhythmical liberties (or "rubatos") with the tempo, which is marked ♩ = 72. These subtle liberties are what make a relaxed and unmechanical interpretation to this opening section.

The piano should start the introduction at a rather full dynamic level but again very smooth and connected, and gradually diminish to a "piano" (p) as the soloist enters in measure 4.

The soloist should note that the solo opens with a straight mute and at a soft dynamic level. Again, a reminder of the great importance of observing the dynamic contrasts, such as the slight crescendo in measures 4 and 5 and the diminuendo in measure 6. It is equally important that the accompanist observe the dynamic indications to adequately furnish chordal support to the soloist.

In measure 4, the ties over the bar-line in the piano accompaniment indicate that the accompanist should allow the chord at measure 4 to sustain through into measure 5. In measure 8, the solo part becomes more dramatic by means of a gradual ascending melodic line coupled with a gradual crescendo into the high "A♭". Remember that "A♭" is the enharmonic of "G♯" and should be fingered the same.

Many of the breath marks in this solo have been placed in parentheses (') indicating optional breath marks — that is, breathe only if necessary, but take the breath as quickly as possible to avoid interrupting the continuity of the melodic line.

Measures 13-25   In measure 13, the tempo should become more strict, (♩ =72) without the rhythmic liberties suggested in the earlier part of the solo. The accompanist should note the "LH" indications in measures 13 to 16, indicating this note should be played with the left hand. In measure 17, the "simile" indicates a continuation of this fingering.

The soloist should have removed the mute during the three measure rest. For the entrance at measure 17, be sure you have your lip set for the "F♯", with plenty of air so this beautiful melodic section can be played with a well-projected sound. Take care to observe the dynamic "inflections" Be very careful to observe the slurs as they are written. Avoid any tendency to shorten the last note of each of the slurred patterns — give the last note of each slur its full value before proceeding into the next slurred figure.

Measures 26-46   In measure 26 and following, the accompanist should play the quarter notes in the right hand very connected as indicated by the term "legato". The soloist must be very careful to keep the eighth note melody beginning at measure 27 very even, avoiding any tendency to rush the tempo. Again, in the section starting at measure 33, the slurred indications are rather irregular, but important to the interpretation of the melody.

Starting at measure 34, both the soloist and accompanist start a gradual build-up to a dramatic climax-point, ending with the soloist's sustained "F♯" in measure 37. Do not hesitate to break the slur for the optional breath at measure 35 if you feel you need the breath to play the sustained "F♯" at a powerful and well-controlled "forte". The musical tension which has been built up to measure 37 should not be allowed to lessen, but continues on through the soloist's re-entrance at measure 40. Only at measure 44 will the excitement of this section begin to subside to a dynamic level (in measure 46) that corresponds to that at the beginning of the solo.

Measures 47-61   At measure 46, the accompanist sets the stylistic and dynamic mood for a re-entrance of the muted trumpet which is reminiscent of the trumpet's original opening statement at measure 5. The soloist can again take a little more rhythmic freedom from measure 51 to the end of the solo. Especially at measure 58, the soloist should feel a gradual subsiding of both tempo and volume and the accompanist should strive to play the last chords, from measure 59 to the end, very softly and with much delicacy.

If the accompanist does not have enough "finger-reach" in the left hand to play the final chord (measure 61), this chord may be "rolled". The accompanist should also note the fermata over the quarter rest in measure 61, indicating the final half-note chord on the third count should be slightly delayed.

"So Soft the Silver Sound and Clear"

Introducing Dr. Robert Getchell

As an educator, clinician, performer, and author, Dr. Getchell ranks in the forefront of brass instrumental specialists and has made noteworthy contributions to the cause of music education. Prior to his present appointment at Luther College, his career in instrumental education has included pubic school teaching in Iowa as well as faculty positions at East Carolina State University, Bowling Green State University, and the Jordan College of Music of Butler University in Indianapolis. He has performed with symphony and studio orchestras and has served as clinician for the Selmer Corporation. He is a frequent and welcome clinician at state music educator and regional MENC meetings.

In addition to this trumpet text and recording, Dr. Getchell's publications include several etude books for the brass instruments and a textbook designed for college brass method classes. He holds a master's degree from the Eastman School of Music and a doctorate from the State University of Iowa.

This series of solos was specifically designed to conform with the requirements of the many Solo and Ensemble Contest Festivals. They have been chosen so that each piece will present to the adjudicator the elements of performance so necessary to a correct evaluation. The time limitation is also a consideration so the length of each has been structured in the two to four minute length.

More specifically, the material had the following objectives:

1. To present highest quality music from the Baroque, Classical, Romantic, Impressionistic, and Contemporary periods.
2. To keep the difficulty of the solos within the technical limits of this particular level.
3. To select solos which could improve your artistic and technical capabilities.
4. To present in each piece some examples of the principal categories of the grading, such as Tone Quality, Intonation, Technic, Rhythm, Articulation, and Interpretation.

Dr. Charles Geyer, of the Chicago Symphony, will perform each solo on the recording. He will be accompanied by Mr. Sheldon Shkolnik, professional piano soloist and accompanist.

It is our hope that you'll enjoy this innovative approach to music study and development. The care in preparation is of course the prime factor in successful presentation.

fingering chart

(Notes in grey are not taught in this book.)